Report

A Torn Safety Net:
How the cost of living crisis threatens its own last line of defence

Hannah Rich

Foreword by Gordon Brown and Dr Rowan Williams

A Torn Safety Net

Foreword

For the first time not just in our lifetimes but since the welfare state was created, we have seen that it is the food bank, not social security, that has become our safety net, and charity, not Universal Credit, that has been the last line of defence. Yet, just as need rises, now comes evidence in this report by the think tank Theos that the UK's faith and voluntary sectors find themselves as precarious as the people they are helping.

Compassion, of course, is not running out but cash is. Donors who have had a little and have generously given to those who have nothing are now finding themselves unable to give at all, and some of those who have donated to food banks are now themselves relying on them. Even churches, which have selflessly offered their heated halls to help vulnerable people stay warm, know they will struggle to pay their own fuel bills, as this report starkly demonstrates.

The shocking reality is that this winter, we are likely to see charities being forced to stop feeding the hungry so they can help the starving, cut back on support to the poorly housed so they can focus on the fast-rising numbers of homeless, and give up on helping the down-at-heel because their priority has to be the destitute.

It is often said that a society is judged by how it treats its most vulnerable members. Faith communities will see it as an essential element of their calling and witness to remind all of us of this. But it is also crucial to remember that the failure to act compassionately and effectively today will build up worse problems for tomorrow – in this, as in so many other areas. It may seem tempting not to notice just how serious the situation is; but we cannot afford – economically or morally – to inflict fresh burdens on our children and grandchildren.

What we are waiting to hear from the latest administration in Westminster is whether this urgency is recognized, and whether there is enough honesty abut the problem and enough willingness to find a solution. Britain's safety net is torn. So much is clear from this report. We dare to hope that it is not torn beyond repair; but that is up to public as well as private vision and generosity.

Gordon Brown, former prime minister

Dr Rowan Williams, former Archbishop of Canterbury

November 2022

Contents

Contents

This report in 60 seconds	**8**
Acknowledgements	**10**
Introduction	**12**
Defining insecurity	**19**
Insecurity in 2022	**26**
A social recession	**52**
Recommendations	**79**

This report in 60 seconds

This report in 60 seconds

The COVID-19 pandemic and the rising cost of living have made life acutely less secure for many people. This level of chronic insecurity has been growing over the longer term, however, and the collective impact of household insecurity is beginning to show in whole communities. It is no longer a crisis only of individual circumstances, but a systemic problem, reflected in the fraying fabric of civil society and faith groups. These institutions form a vital part of the safety net, offering security and material support to millions of people, but are themselves becoming less secure. There is a risk that churches and other faith groups will close, not because of falling attendance or religious affiliation, but because they cannot afford to keep the lights on.

This report details the scale and scope of this issue, which we argue constitutes an emerging "social recession". It is critical that community and faith groups are supported and secured both during and beyond the current crisis, and to this end we offer policy recommendations which focus on systemic as well as individual insecurity. We argue also that there is a strong theological rationale for taking insecurity seriously as a socio-economic issue, distinct from poverty, rooted in the Old Testament.

# Acknowledgements

I would like to thank my Theos colleagues for their support throughout this research, in particular: Simon Perfect, who recruited participants and conducted a large number of interviews; Wendy Appenteng Daniels, who assisted with interviews and observations; Paul Bickley, who helped steer the research in the best direction; and Nick Spencer and Marianne Rozario, who provided feedback on various drafts. I would also like to thank Pete Whitehead, who first suggested precarity as a research topic, and Ben Ryan for his incredibly valuable comments on an early draft.

This report would also not have been possible without the contributions of the individuals, organisations, and communities who generously took part in the research. We are grateful to them all for sharing so honestly about their experiences at such a challenging time. A particular thanks to Jon Miles, who was instrumental in facilitating the Wolverhampton case study.

Lastly, thank you to the Sir Halley Stewart Trust for funding this research.

Hannah Rich, November 2022

Introduction

This is not the report we set out to write. At its conception, this research aimed to explore how "precarity", a category of socio-economic insecurity coined by economist Guy Standing,[1] might affect how people relate to faith communities and other groups.

If someone's economic life is precarious, does that mean they might struggle to remain part of faith communities, or could faith act as an anchor and a point of stability?

What does it look like to hold community together when the majority of people in a congregation are on zero-hours contracts, or in shift work, and their time isn't fully their own?

Would precarity hinder the build-up of supportive relationships within communities – what we refer to as social capital[2] – and of networks of shared faith and values – spiritual capital?[3]

We formulated these questions in summer 2021, before the onset of the cost of living crisis in the UK[4] and the war in Ukraine. Over the course of this project our collective and individual lives have undeniably

There are very few people whose economic situation is not now more fragile than it was.

become less secure. By the time interviews began in January 2022, the economy was becoming more unstable; we were already conscious that the proportion of the population experiencing economic insecurity had increased. Without diminishing the particular circumstances of the "precariat", as Standing coined it, there are very few people whose economic situation is not now more fragile than it was. As individual and household situations became ever more insecure, the value of the material support offered by faith groups and other third sector institutions, in addition to the social and spiritual capital they hold, grew.

As the economy has spiralled, we have seen these anchor institutions themselves become less secure. Soaring energy costs threaten the ability to run vital community spaces. At the same time, volunteer capacity is stretched thin and financial donations are drying up. It is a perfect storm. Insecurity is no longer only about individual circumstances, if it ever was, but now a reflection of the fraying fabric of civil society and faith groups.

The matter of how precarity and insecurity affects people's faith engagements remains pertinent, but when asked about how economic insecurity affects their congregation or community, we found that interviewees held both material and spiritual aspects together. They would point to the growing queues at their food bank, or the increased demand for other material support, and connect it to the life of their community in spiritual and social aspects. Our research evolved accordingly.

The report begins by offering a snapshot of how insecurity is affecting the individuals and communities interviewed in the research, including the plethora of forms it takes, from housing and finance to employment and access to food. We view this through both sociological and theological lenses, conceptualising insecurity as broader than just the economy. We explore what the aggregate effect of individual insecurity is for local communities and congregations, and

> **If nothing is done to alleviate the effects at an organisational level, the UK third sector could well experience a "social recession".**

its consequences in both practical and spiritual terms. We track what this means for faith groups and charities, arguing that if nothing is done to alleviate the effects at an organisational level, the UK third sector could well experience a "social recession" alongside the impending economic recession.

As insecurity moves from the individual to the systemic, and from the chronic to the acute, this may affect how people express their religious faith and how they engage with voluntary organisations. The next year will see some faith institutions close their doors forever. This will not be because of falling attendance, secularisation, or the perceived irrelevance of religion but because they cannot afford to keep the lights on or find enough volunteers to sustain their social action. The impact of this within communities will be far wider than just those who practise a faith themselves.

The next year will see some faith institutions close their doors forever... because they cannot afford to keep the lights on.

If churches and community groups have the potential to anchor people in otherwise unstable times, it is vital that these collective institutions themselves are supported and secured. We therefore conclude with a series of practical recommendations and policy proposals which we believe are critical to preserving this valuable community safety net, and thus offering greater spiritual and economic security to the wider population.

Methodology

This report is informed by a series of 48 semi-structured interviews conducted by Theos researchers between January and August 2022. These were concentrated in four local authority areas: Cornwall, Glasgow, Wolverhampton, and the London borough of Newham. These areas were selected based on data for various indicators of insecurity, including metrics for housing, debt, and (un)employment, as well as covering both urban and rural areas. Additionally, we interviewed a number of individuals from outside these geographical areas, chosen because of their experience and expertise of particular aspects of insecurity and religion. In each chosen case study area, we interviewed a range of local faith leaders, congregation members, charity workers, community activists, and local government stakeholders. We also considered three other boroughs as case studies, including one in Wales, but received limited response to participant recruitment in those areas. Data and quotes from the single preliminary interview we conducted in each of these three areas are included here but not identified geographically.

Of those interviewed, 17 (35%) were faith leaders, both lay and ordained, recognised in their particular denomination. A further 17 (35%) were leaders or representatives of faith-based charities or civil society groups. Eight (17%) were interviewed in their capacity as leaders or members of local public institutions, such as local government, although several of these had a faith personally. Others were academics, with specific expertise in the topic, or authority-wide stakeholders.

The majority of the participants (70%) identified as Christian, within which 12 different church denominations and non-denominational groups were represented. The other 30% included participants from the Muslim, Jewish, Buddhist, and Bahá'í faiths, as well as a number of individuals who did not identify as part of any faith or belief group. (We tried actively to recruit participants from both Sikh and Hindu faith communities but were unsuccessful.)

Researchers also conducted observations and informal conversations in three congregations or communities involved in the research; two in East London and one in Glasgow.

1. Standing, G, The Precariat: *The New Dangerous Class* (London: Bloomsbury Academic, 2011).

2. See for example: Putnam, R, *Bowling Alone: The Collapse and Revival of American Community* (New York: Simon and Schuster, 2000).

3. Malloch, T R, "Spiritual Capital" in Oslington, P (ed), *The Oxford Handbook of Christianity and Economics* (Oxford: Oxford Academic, 2014). Available at: https://doi.org/10.1093/oxfordhb/9780199729715.013.024

4. Hourston, P, "Cost of living crisis", *Institute for Government* (2022). Available at: www.instituteforgovernment.org.uk/explainers/cost-living-crisis

Defining insecurity

Whether it is energy prices, mortgage rates, or the cost of a regular grocery shop, almost every part of everyday economic activity has become not only more expensive but also less guaranteed over the last 12 months. Amid recent market volatility, the value of the pound has "fallen off a cliff"[1], "tumbled"[2], or "continues to sink"[3] – metaphors which all reflect the unstable economic foundation on which we find ourselves. In the wake of the COVID-19 pandemic, which also destabilised many aspects of daily life, this has led to a growing sense of life in general seeming less secure than it did even a year ago. While there are clear connections with concepts of poverty, inequality, and deprivation, this report focuses on insecurity as a distinct experience. In defining this, therefore, it is important to include the feeling of it in qualitative terms as well as any measurable indicators.

Economic insecurity has been defined as "the anxiety produced by the possible exposure to adverse economic events and by the anticipation of the difficulty to recover from them."[4] This captures the impact on wellbeing of uncertain financial circumstances. Similarly, the RSA defines economic security as "the degree of confidence that a person can have in maintaining a decent quality of life, now and in the future, given their economic and financial circumstances."[5] The future/anticipatory element of both these definitions is critical, particularly when the economy is changing as fast as it is at present.

Some participants felt that insecurity was a helpful term here, because it captured the existential and emotional uncertainty as well as the volatility of people's economic circumstances and their resilience to economic shocks:

"It conveys exactly the situation of not being sure what is going to happen, whether things are going to get better or if they're going to get worse." (Church leader, Glasgow, March 2022)

For example, rising inflation and bills mean that many of those currently able to afford basic necessities like gas, electricity, and groceries cannot be certain they will still be able to do so in several months' time. Even those with a good salary and secure employment status are no longer certain that it will cover the basics of life as inflation continues to rise and the cold weather arrives.

As events in autumn 2022 have shown, the markets do not react well to general financial uncertainty either. Changes to mortgage rates mean that many of those households with the apparent security of owning their home may not be able to meet the repayments; this will be especially acute for the poorest households and recent first-time buyers.[6] In other words, it is a problem not only that thousands of households will experience greater absolute poverty but also that fewer and fewer people can be sure that they will not also fall into that group.

> **Even those with a good salary and secure employment status are no longer certain that it will cover the basics of life as inflation continues to rise.**

While Guy Standing's description of precarity was instrumental in our early thinking for this research, we adopted a broader concept of insecurity. Standing identifies seven dimensions of precarity, from income to education, but all of these are focused heavily on the labour market.[7] We note in particular that this excludes non-labour forms of insecurity, such as housing, personal debt, and savings. Young graduate professionals, for example, might experience precarious housing circumstances within the private rental sector, and low levels of personal savings, but with levels of education and income that are comparatively comfortable.

The lack of a secure work-based identity or control over one's time and resources are less quantifiable but equally important social dimensions of insecurity. It is worth noting that even since Standing first articulated this a decade ago, the forms of insecurity at play within the labour market have further evolved. For instance, neither Uber nor Deliveroo operated in the UK at the time he was writing, nor had the gig economy emerged fully. Accordingly, the number of workers on zero-hours contracts in the UK has increased from 190,000 in 2011 to 990,000 in 2020.[8]

These are all aspects that are critical in differentiating insecurity from poverty, unemployment, or deprivation, as our qualitative research (outlined in the next chapter) found.

It is clear that insecurity cannot be reduced either to material poverty or the nature of the labour market. It is also a social phenomenon, linked to a lack of predictability across a range of factors including employment, income, housing, community, and relationship. It can be induced or exacerbated by weak or fragmented public services and the absence of stabilising social relations. If we have a framework that only captures the economic factors, we are unlikely to accurately document insecurity or bring the necessary resources into play in tackling it.

It is worth saying that many faith traditions instinctively focus more on these relational aspects of disadvantage. For example, there are clear parallels with how socio-economic challenges are framed in the core texts of both Jewish and

Christian faiths. As well as valuable religious texts, these are also historical examples of societies acknowledging insecurity as a key issue.

The legal codes laid out in the Torah and the Old Testament repeatedly highlight the plight of widows, orphans, and foreigners, alongside the more general category of "the poor".[9] These groups are often bracketed together as those for whom there is a moral responsibility to care, although their circumstances are different. They are defined variously by their financial position, their status as stranger, and by the loss of stability linked to the loss of a male relative. What unites them is that they are all socially insecure groups, without the connections within society that would allow them to flourish. All of them found themselves outside the extended household units.[10] These extended households performed economic, welfare-protective, and spiritual/religious/educational roles in Old Testament Israel. To be detached from them was to be deprived of a range of goods and therefore rendered objectively and subjectively insecure or vulnerable.

There is also provision and an explicit responsibility for the security of one's neighbours. A Jewish participant in our research cited Deuteronomy 22:8, which instructs the building of a parapet on the roof of any new house, so that no one can fall off. It was suggested that this might also imply the construction of societal safeguards so that no one could similarly "fall off" the economy. Similarly, Catholic Social Teaching directly recognises the way that the multiple forms of stability and security are interlinked. One cannot have stable family life without stable housing, one cannot have stable housing without stable employment, one cannot have stable employment without a stable economy, and one cannot have a stable economy without a stable state.[11]

In defining a concept of insecurity as broader than just the economic, therefore, we also envisioned life as something richer than just its economic value. The social and spiritual aspects of life are fundamental to human wellbeing, and the ways they are affected by insecurity are therefore important to consider too, as we go on to explore further.

The social and spiritual aspects of life are fundamental to human wellbeing, and the ways they are affected by insecurity are therefore important.

We begin by outlining what we see as four key facets of insecurity, drawn from the experiences of the individuals and communities in our research, along with how faith communities can mitigate this through relationship and stability. We then describe how this is affecting communities and charities at a wider level, arguing that this constitutes a social recession. We conclude with a series of recommendations to government, the charity sector, and faith groups for how they can address this.

1 Withers, P, "Pound 'falling off cliff' against dollar in 'tragic year for sterling' after crisis budget", *Daily Express*, 24 September 2022. Available at: www.express.co.uk/finance/city/1673292/Pound-to-euro-exchange-dollar-live-latest-FTSE-updates-budget-statement-today-UK-energy

2 Nolsøe, E, "How the tumbling pound is pushing up prices", the *Telegraph*, 29 September 2020. Available at: www.telegraph.co.uk/business/2022/09/29/how-tumbling-pound-pushing-prices/

3 Cohen, P, "Why the British Pound Continues to Sink", *The New York Times*, 28 September 2022. Available at: www.nytimes.com/2022/09/28/business/economy/uk-pound-history.html

4 Bossert, W and C D'Ambrosio, "Measuring economic insecurity", *International Economic Review*, 54(3) (2013), pp. 1017–1030.

5 Shafique, A, *Addressing Economic Inequality* (London: RSA, 2018). Available at: www.thersa.org/globalassets/pdfs/reports/rsa-addressing-economic-insecurity.pdf

6 Thomas, H, "Where this UK mortgage meltdown will really bite", *Financial Times*, 28 September 2022. Available at: www.ft.com/content/1795e739-6e11-43cd-bf92-d7d2ad0324b2

7 Standing, *The Precariat*, p. 11.

8 Statista Data, *Number of employees on a zero-hours contract in the United Kingdom from 2000 to 2021* (2021). Available at: www.statista.com/statistics/414896/employees-with-zero-hours-contracts-number/

9 For example, Isaiah 1:17, Zechariah 7:10, and Deuteronomy 10:18, among many other verses, all mention these groups of people in various translations.

10 As an aside, Deuteronomy 14:28–29 also includes the Levite class – "who have no allotment or inheritance of their own" (NIV) – in this list of vulnerable groups.

11 See §1909 of the Catechism of the Catholic Church.

6
Insecurity in 2022

In order to understand insecurity more comprehensively as a qualitative experience, not only a combination of socio-economic indicators, we interviewed people in faith communities in four case study areas. We identified these areas as particularly insecure, whether due to the proportion of rented housing locally or the level of personal and household debt. These quantitative data were used as a starting point, but we did not want to assume that they captured the full extent or nature of insecurity in a place. We therefore began each interview open-endedly by asking participants to describe what the reality of insecurity looks and feels like for them and their community.

> *"The sense is that as a country, although we're being told lots of feelgood stories, the reality on the ground is that the whole thing feels quite uncertain. You've got that going on within communities. It has the potential to change the narrative slightly around attitudes to money and the poor, because a lot more people are feeling uncertain, not least when you have the contrast with extreme displays of wealth as well."* (Community worker, Wolverhampton, February 2022)

This was insightful not only in finding out how people understood the term but also in tracking how it changed over the course of the research. The earliest interviewees, speaking in mid-January 2022, barely mentioned the cost of living crisis, and were more likely to discuss various forms of insecurity in the context of the waning pandemic. They were also generally less gloomy about the outlook, to an extent that appears almost naïve in light of subsequent geopolitical and economic events. By contrast, by the time we reached the final interview in early August 2022, the question of what insecurity feels and looks like could not be considered in isolation from the intensifying cost of living crisis. Later in the research, it was also harder to disentangle the specific experience of insecurity from that of disadvantage, poverty, or increasingly dire economic circumstances.

> *"The majority of my congregation are economically insecure. That's a variety of things, from people who are living in multiple occupancy places, asylum seeker houses, to people who have no recourse to public funds, or migrants who are perhaps working, to families who've begun to establish a life for themselves."*
> (Vicar, Wolverhampton, May 2022)

Some were quick to emphasise the long-term, chronic nature of insecurity in their context, albeit exacerbated and made more acute by current events. Particularly early in the research, and therefore early in our understanding of the scale of the economic crisis facing the country, several interviewees suggested that the cost of living crisis was "nothing new" for them. One community worker even suggested that "insecurity" was perhaps too tentative a word for the circumstances of people with whom they work, because "insecurity" implies being on the verge of something as opposed to the full-blown crisis situation which is a common reality for their clients.

> *"Economic insecurity is all sorts of things. I would say it is existence in the 21st century in this area… It's very difficult to identify anybody [here] who hasn't been hit by greater economic insecurity during the last few years…*
>
> *For me, I suppose it's not a sense of something that's happened, because the cost of living crisis has always been here. What I would say is that the cost of living crisis has deepened and it's getting to extents that are actually shocking in the sense of how little people are able to manage where they would have been able to perhaps get by before."* (Vicar, Wolverhampton, May 2022)

Growing food bank use, long-term unemployment, low pay, and a reduced welfare state capacity have been constant realities for the best part of a decade, but the severity of their combined effects on community and economic resilience were unrealised for many until now. The doubling of energy bills in the last 12 months in particular has brought this into the wider public imagination, affecting even those who were relatively unscathed by years of austerity.

According to polling from Ipsos, net optimism about the general economic condition of the country is at its lowest in 2022 since the 2008 economic crisis, despite the fact that the intervening period has been marked by significant insecurity for many of the population.[1] This is a psychological point as much as it is an economic or political one. If insecurity is characterised by anxiety about adverse economic events and the anticipation of a difficult recovery from them, as Bossert and D'Ambrosio suggest, then it is certainly true that it has become more widespread recently.[2] Polling on the cost of living conducted by Public First in early September 2022 found that, when asked about the future looking ahead to next year, 53% of people were either very or quite pessimistic.[3] Anxiety and economic pessimism have both risen this year, even if the individual components that contribute to economic insecurity have long been rising.

From our research, we identify four key dimensions of insecurity: income and employment; housing; access to food; and migration status. These emerged as the most common facets of insecurity identified and experienced by participants, as well as having clear relevance to faith

We identify four key dimensions of insecurity: income and employment; housing; access to food; and migration status.

communities. Each of these dimensions represents something of the Old Testament categories of orphan, widow, and alien, and they represent both economic and non-economic aspects of insecurity. We now describe each of these in turn, as well as outlining how they each can and do affect how people interact with their faith communities and practise their faith.

Insecurity of income and employment

For many participants, insecurity was described initially in terms of personal and household finances, through insecure income, debt, and savings. This was frequently connected to insecure employment conditions and a lack of job security. The COVID-19 pandemic revealed much of this latent insecurity, and its public health implications. For example, having savings offered a degree of financial security when required to self-isolate when diagnosed with the coronavirus. Those with less than £100 in savings, or an income under £20,000, were seen to be three times less likely to be able to successfully self-isolate if required to.[4] Furthermore, the ability of key workers to take time off in the event of illness was correlated to their financial position. Research by the RSA found that social care workers in particular have lower levels of savings with which to absorb unexpected unpaid time, but are also less likely to have adequate structural support (e.g. paid leave) if and when they are forced to take time out of work.[5] One in five key workers said they would struggle to do so, which rose to 47% of those who would also struggle to pay an unexpected bill of £100.[6]

Household debt often arises from the financial instability of not knowing what your income will be from month to month, coupled with limited structural support or access to other financial means. Debt advice centres operated by churches mitigate this, but their staff and volunteers are well aware of the mental health impact of insecurity, and the vicious circle it represents. One debt advisor told us that their first port of call used to be to help people find the best possible energy deal to reduce their household outgoings and thus address problem debt, but that that is now "an absolute joke".

"By the time you get into debt, you're fairly insecure. When you come and ask for help, you're desperate... I think debt and insecurity are synonymous really, especially for more vulnerable people like those we tend to work with." (Debt advisor, Wolverhampton, May 2022)

With regard to finance, insecurity also breeds insecurity in the sense that without a secure income, it is harder to access affordable forms of credit that might help people improve their circumstances. Low savings and limited access to credit combine to reduce an individual's resilience to economic shocks. Take for example if your car breaks down unexpectedly. If you don't have savings available to pay for repairs and also do not have a secure enough financial position to borrow from mainstream lenders, you either borrow from less reputable forms of credit, or simply do without a car. This might affect your ability to travel to work, which in turn is likely to increase insecurity and related anxiety, and could worsen your credit position, beginning the cycle again.

There is a theological as well as practical precedent for churches speaking about security of both work and income.

Faith communities have been instrumental in campaigns against pay-day lending and for better working conditions. The concept of the "living wage" can be traced through a number of Papal Encyclicals, representing over 100 years of the Catholic Church's teaching. As early as 1862, Pope Leo XIII wrote in his encyclical *Rerum Novarum* that a worker's wages should "be sufficient to enable him comfortably to support himself, his wife, and his children".[7] There is a theological as well as practical precedent for churches speaking about security of both work and income.

Most recently, campaigns have coalesced around the idea of "living hours" as well as a living wage as a way of providing greater security for workers. The irregularity of working hours is often the driver for insecure and precarious working practices which negatively impact employees, in particular those on the lowest incomes.[8] This reflects the fact that for many, income insecurity is inherently linked to the insecurity of their employment itself. In recent decades, greater productivity has emerged as the defining aim of government policy around the labour market, at the expense of emphasising the quality of jobs. This has brought with it an increase in jobs with insecure conditions and low pay.

The rise of the gig economy, for example, is a political and societal choice not an economic inevitability. It is a choice with clear consequences for job and employment insecurity, as was highlighted throughout the research.

One Anglican priest in East London spoke about how you can physically see what precariousness or insecurity looks like in the groups of migrant workers who congregate outside warehouses and DIY stores around her parish, hoping to be collected by contractors in vans and offered a day's work for minimal pay. She drew the parallel between this and the practice of "standing on the stones", which was also prevalent in East London historically, whereby dockworkers would arrive at the docks first thing in the morning in hope of employment that day. This practice disappeared with the advent of employment laws, which saw these jobs on the docks become contractual when the Dock Workers (Regulation of Employment) Act was passed in 1946. However, this has not regulated insecurity out of the economy altogether and the

Precarious economic positions of the dockers have re-emerged, manifested in the car parks of industrial estates a few miles away.

precarious economic positions of the dockers have re-emerged, manifested in the car parks of industrial estates a few miles away. (It was also pointed out that Jesus describes a similar practice in the parable of the labourers in the vineyard, told in Matthew 20, which sees the landowner go out early in the morning to hire workers for that day. While it is used as a parable about mercy and justice, it perhaps demonstrates how Jesus was awake to the insecurity of prevalent employment practices in his time.)

Another priest gave the example of an Eastern European family in their congregation, whose father has a professional occupation and a reasonably good salary but is employed by government subcontractors on rolling temporary or short-term contracts. The number of people in involuntary temporary contracts – those who cannot find permanent work, rather than those who have chosen the flexibility of temporary arrangements – rose significantly over the course of the pandemic.[9] Even for many of those in paid employment, work life is thus transient and unstable.

"If you don't know when the work is coming, if today you work and tomorrow the work is not there, then how are you going to meet your financial needs? It makes your life unstable because

you don't know whether you're going or coming. If it's constant, then you know where your money will come from and then you know when you'll be able to give some time to volunteer or do something for somebody else." (Pastor, Newham, May 2022)

As with housing, job insecurity is often self-perpetuating. Without having secure housing or income, it is often more difficult to achieve secure housing or income, and this can become cyclical. If life is insecure, it may be harder to find time, energy, or physical space for education, for example. The lack of education may then reinforce the inability to achieve a better-paid job which would render secure housing attainable, and so on, and so on. We heard from the founder of a social enterprise working with migrant factory workers in the particularly precarious garment industry about how the workers could not afford to learn English because it would constitute "unpaid" work time, which neither they nor their employers could cover. This in turn left them trapped in the precarious industry without the language skills to find a more secure source of income or improve their living circumstances.

> **Without having secure housing or income, it is often more difficult to achieve secure housing or income, and this can become cyclical.**

There are also disparities between ethnic and religious groups in terms of the experience of insecure employment. A representative of a national Muslim charity spoke about how people in their communities had been impacted more severely by the economic effects of the pandemic, because they are more likely to be self-employed or working in retail or hospitality. According to the Runnymede Trust, a quarter of Black, Asian, or Minority Ethnic (BAME) workers have gig economy jobs, compared to 14% of the general population.[10] These jobs are typically classed as self-employed and do not provide a guaranteed income, nor were they covered by the emergency support packages provided by the UK government. Participants highlighted that there may be religious reasons why certain demographics choose particular occupations, or perceived benefits to more flexible employment; for example, for some Muslim men, working as a taxi driver affords the flexibility to attend Friday prayers in the middle of the working day. However, the insecurity in these professions further entrenches the insecurity of those demographic groups.

Those in industries like retail or hospitality were also affected; nearly one in three Bangladeshi men in the UK work in restaurants, compared to one in 100 White British men.[11] The temporary closure of these businesses during lockdown pushed these individuals, most of whom are Muslim, further into financial insecurity, with data suggesting that BAME workers were more likely than White workers to have been made redundant rather than placed on the furlough scheme.[12]

These trends are likely to worsen if the economic crisis and energy price rise lead to the permanent closure of many small businesses in the hospitality sector. This will only intensify the widespread insecurity of both income and employment that we have seen to be a significant issue.

Housing insecurity

Housing-related insecurity was another common theme among participants and was, at least prior to the energy crisis, the form of insecurity which affected the widest demographic, cutting across income brackets and educational backgrounds. For example, the insecurity that comes with living in a rented property is as tangible if you are a private tenant on a professional salary as if you are a social housing tenant. For many renters, your home is only as secure as the landlord's intentions, especially in areas where there is a limited supply regardless of your ability to pay.

> *"It goes back to your very identity... If you're going from one tenancy to another, you can't really put down roots. You might want to join the community and the local church, but then your landlord gives you notice and you're moved to somewhere else. I think it leads you to not know who you are or where you are."*
> (Church leader, Glasgow, February 2022)

One of our case study areas was Cornwall, where this is particularly acute. Holiday rentals and second homes account for a large proportion of the Cornish housing market, to the detriment of local people. During the pandemic, the situation was exacerbated by the rise in second homeowners, UK holidaymakers, and city dwellers taking advantage of the growth of working from home. In June 2021, it was reported that there were 10,000 properties available as short-term holiday lets and fewer than 50 for long-term tenancies, a statistic that three separate participants quoted to us unprompted.[13] Waiting lists for social housing in Cornwall almost doubled between 2020 and 2022.[14]

Nationally, homelessness due to no-fault eviction – known as a section 21 – was up 37% in 2021 on pre-pandemic levels.[15] Anecdotally, this is a particular problem in Cornwall. All those we interviewed in the region had stories from their own lives or of people in their communities who had had to move house against their will. In many cases, this was due to a no-fault eviction because the landlord wanted to sell or put the property up for more lucrative holiday rental.

This is destabilising for the whole community, not only in economic terms. Residents who own their own homes still spoke about the detrimental impact on the sense of community and identity locally and on the weakening of cohesive relationships as a result.

"It has really affected the sense of community. One of the things with the pandemic is that all these rich Londoners are coming down and buying up property. The cost of property has rocketed over the last two or three years. That's not just the economic thing... It's the sense of property and not being the absolute owner of where you live, not having a relationship with the people around you." (Community leader, Cornwall, May 2022)

Another aspect of housing insecurity we observed was the quality of housing, where problems often stem from insecure income and may be cyclical. Insecure monthly income, for example, may be considered negatively by landlords or creditors, leaving people to resort to less scrupulous housing providers or poorer quality accommodation. We heard how this results in overcrowded housing, particularly in inner city areas. The proportion of socially and private rented households classed as overcrowded has risen in recent years, to the highest levels since data collection began.[16] The two constituencies with the highest rates of household overcrowding at the last census both fell into our case study borough of Newham.[17] A lay leader from one church congregation in the research described sharing a single room in a house in multiple occupation (HMO) with his family, including four small children. He has to leave for work at anti-social hours, leading to sleep deprivation for all the family.

Participants spoke about how overcrowding and poor housing affects people's health and morale, with consequences for their family life, mental health, education, and employment status. A survey by the National Housing Federation echoed this, finding that nearly a third of Britons experienced health problems due to conditions or lack of space in their homes during the COVID-19 lockdowns.[18] Housing instability has a demonstrable impact on relationships; recent research found that there is no part of the UK where a single woman on average income can afford to rent the median home. There are also recorded cases of rental contracts with "no children" clauses, which has a palpable impact on family life as well as removing the general feeling of control over one's own life decisions.[19]

> **Housing instability has a demonstrable impact on relationships.**

Several participants described how families living in overcrowded accommodation or without any outdoor space valued their church, mosque, or community centre as a building where there is space for their children to run around safely and freely. However, this also relates back to the insecurity of the whole faith community. Overcrowding affects ethnic minority households more than White British households,[20] and minority religious groups and denominations are in turn often reliant on rented spaces rather than dedicated places of worship and therefore do not necessarily have access to these spaces outside of Sunday worship.

Conversely, we heard elsewhere how when secure housing does exist, it has a significant impact on how secure life feels more generally. One community organiser in the north west of England articulated this well. Her community is classed among the most deprived in the country and ranks poorly for community wellbeing. Unlike most of the country, the social housing stock in the town is still owned and run by the council and is plentiful. While life is difficult for many people, she spoke about how several generations of the same family might have lived in the same council property and therefore have a secure and stable sense of home, which is a totally different experience to people in equally deprived urban areas elsewhere in the country. Similarly, there are two large main employers in the town, which provide low-paid but stable employment, and so while there is deprivation arising from low pay and low levels of education, unemployment is not a prominent concern.

"I lived in London for years and housing insecurity was a massive thing and so directly related to the experience of poverty there in a way that just isn't the case here... It's interesting because I've always thought of poverty as related to precariousness, and yet there's almost something quite secure about generational poverty." (Organiser, March 2022)

Secure housing therefore has a positive impact on overall security and wellbeing, even where finance, income, or access to food remain insecure. However, in many areas, the price and unavailability of housing make it hard for local families and younger people to stay in the area, with negative consequences for the whole community. When young families are priced out of an area, local faith congregations and community groups often have ageing memberships, which may not be sustainable and is a source of sadness or even loss. A member of

> **In many areas, the price and unavailability of housing make it hard for local families and younger people to stay in the area.**

the Jewish community in Cornwall spoke powerfully about how
the lack of children and young families, attributed directly to
the local housing market, was something that would negatively
impact their collective ability to practise some of the rituals
and festivals of the Jewish faith, for which children are a key
part:

> *"One of the central lessons that we're given in the Torah is to
> teach what we know to our children, to hand it down. Children
> are central to the festival of Pesach. They are involved in the
> ritual of it. They ask the questions at the heart of Pesach. We
> talk about the importance of memory and handing down that
> memory, but if we don't have any children here, how do we do
> that?"* (Jewish community member, Cornwall, May 2022)

This example encapsulated the finding from many
different faith groups that insecurity – particularly that of
housing – is devastating for communities on the level of
spirituality as well as economy.

More positively, we heard how a young congregation
member who had been served with a section 21 eviction notice
was able to find temporary housing with an older couple in the
church. He reflected that, if not for the church, this would not
have been possible. In motivational terms, the generosity of the
couple to offer up their spare room might be directly attributed
to their faith, but in practical demographic terms, they would
not have met the young person outside of the church. There
was no other social setting in which he could imagine having
had a close existing relationship with a married couple two
generations above him and in a much more secure economic
position.

Faith communities often span social groups and
demographics which would not typically meet in other

settings, as the Social Integration Commission found in 2015.[21] Based on the average age of landlords (or homeowners) and tenants respectively, there are few other social settings where the two are as likely to interact as they are in faith communities. In a community where homeownership and renting are divisive fault lines, the church can bridge this. There are many, more structural ways in which faith communities can challenge housing inequalities, but this was an encouraging example of how belonging to a local congregation can offer some security. Faith communities thus embody relationships of trust and common cultural understanding across societal divides and in doing so, offer solutions to some of the greatest economic insecurities of our time. They matter socially as well as spiritually, and both social and spiritual roles would be missed if they ceased to exist.

> **Faith communities often span social groups and demographics which would not typically meet in other settings.**

Food insecurity

The language of food insecurity has become increasingly prominent in the current crisis. This is defined as the lack of reliable access to a sufficient quantity of affordable, nutritious food, and has replaced "food poverty" as the term commonly used by charities and campaigners working in this space.[22] The Food Foundation found that nearly one in five low-income families experienced food insecurity in September 2022, more than in the first weeks of the COVID-19 lockdown. In the same month, one in four UK households with children reported going an entire day without eating because of the cost.[23] The increasing acute economic challenges have seen more and more people relying on food banks:

> *"I think [people] are far more comfortable going to a mosque and picking up a food parcel now. Before, that would have come with a sense of shame or embarrassment, but necessity has won out."*
> (National charity director, June 2022)

As Stephen Cottrell, the Archbishop of York, said in a speech to the House of Lords in October 2022, many of those who until recently donated to food banks are now having to visit them.[24]

For many communities, food insecurity is nothing new. It has been rising constantly over the last decade; as early as 2014, a report published by the Trussell Trust, Oxfam, and Church Action on Poverty described the rise of food poverty in the UK as "relentless".[25] In 2021-22, the Trussell Trust gave out 2.1 million emergency food parcels, slightly down on 2.3 million the previous year when the pandemic was at its peak, but still up by 81% in the last five years.[26] The proportion of Church of England churches involved in supporting a food bank or similar initiative to address food poverty has more than doubled from 33% in 2011[27] to 78% of parishes in 2021.[28] This reflects the growth in demand for emergency food provision of this sort across the wider community; a recent survey by food charity Magic Breakfast found that 81% of respondent primary schools believe that child hunger has increased in their school communities since 2021.[29]

Several participants described food insecurity in terms of the increased demand at food banks in their community and in particular the growing numbers of people who are in work but still have recourse to food provision. The opening hours of some food banks, now reaching beyond 9-5, reflect this sense that work is not a guarantee of security. Relative poverty among working households rose from 13% in 1996 to 17.4%

in early 2020.[30] For many working people, there is "always more month than money left", as one participant expressed it. During the mourning period after the death of Queen Elizabeth II, there was debate about whether food banks should remain open on the bank holiday, demonstrating the extent to which the service they provide – staffed by volunteers who also deserve to take bank holidays – has been absorbed into everyday life and lost the sense of "emergency" provision it used to carry.[31] This is indicative of the wider way in which voluntary services have become an important part of the fabric of welfare provision, making it doubly concerning that the voluntary sector is itself experiencing insecurity.

> **For many working people, there is "always more month than money left".**

"Food insecurity is a massive problem here, and I think a lot of people are worried about what the cost of living increase is going to do to them because they were already struggling." (Church community worker, Glasgow, March 2022)

The margins between being able to afford food and not were slim for many people even before this crisis. In one community, we heard how a local church had proposed setting up a food pantry, rather than a food bank. This system requires people to pay a membership fee, which then entitles them to pay £3 for a box of food from the pantry, which they are also allowed to choose themselves. The theory behind this is that it affords more dignity than a food bank system where people are given a parcel without choosing the contents. However, for many, the £5 up-front membership fee was not an expense they could necessarily afford, even as early as February 2022. Another community centre had decided not to reopen its café after lockdown because of concerns people couldn't afford it.

"For many people, the concept of anything to fall back on isn't there. When food goes up 5%, that's it. Over the edge." (Food bank volunteer, Wolverhampton, April 2022)

As we will go on to explore later in the report, these inflationary margins are beginning to be passed onto churches, voluntary groups, and food charities themselves, with significant implications for their ability to address food insecurity for those in their communities.

The relational dynamics of food insecurity also became more widespread during the COVID-19 pandemic. If you tested positive for coronavirus the day before you planned to do a weekly grocery shop, for example, then irrespective of your economic security, your access to food was inextricably linked to your relational security. At certain times during the lockdown periods, no amount of money could buy you an online food shopping slot at short notice and you were thus reliant on social networks of friends, neighbours, or relations to deliver food and supplies while you isolated. This was true across all demographic groups and is a striking example of how relative economic advantage does not always negate the social forms of insecurity and even access to food.

> **Having no recourse to public funds is an inherently insecure position, exempting an estimated million individuals from the safety net of the welfare system.**

Refugee and migrant insecurity

In some communities, participants also highlighted the various forms of insecurity linked to migration status, as a long-term experience. This has been amplified further over the course of the research, with the onset of the war in Ukraine leading to almost 100,000 Ukrainian refugees arriving in the UK. Having no recourse to public funds is an inherently insecure position, exempting an estimated million individuals from the safety net of the welfare system.

Growing numbers of asylum seekers from Afghanistan and elsewhere are now housed in insecure and temporary accommodation, including in hotels. At the end of 2021, there were over 26,000 asylum seekers housed in hotels across the country.[32] We heard from several faith groups for whom this is a significant issue in their locality and who were reactively trying to work to support those housed there, while recognising that these placements are often short-term.

The bar set by the government for community sponsorship schemes is reasonably high. Groups wanting to sponsor refugee families have to demonstrate their capacity to offer housing, school places, transport, a support network, and general local goodwill before they reach the beginning of the visa process. They have to raise £9,000 in a designated bank account for sponsorship purposes and the process can take up to 18 months. When it comes to temporary hotel accommodation, the reverse is often true. The placement of vulnerable individuals and families, whether asylum seekers or homeless, in hotels happens at the decision of the Home Office, council departments, or hotel management. The impact on the local community of an entire hotel full of people – often totalling up to 300 families – moving into an area at once, for months or years at a time, is greater than that of one or two families, yet the community infrastructure is often far less prepared. Charitable support from charities and faith groups is reactive by necessity.

With the exception of the Homes for Ukraine programme, families and local communities welcoming refugees do not have to name the specific individual or family they are welcoming. Conversely, in the original Canadian model of community sponsorship, there is an encouragement to build on existing links and networks in identifying a family to sponsor. This builds on connections like a shared faith, which might strengthen relationships, cohesion, and security. One church leader we interviewed in Glasgow had previously worked in Canada and noted the value of this approach:

> *"They journeyed with them every day, supportively not oppressively so, then you would pull back and let go a little. Then you'd have, in a celebratory way, anniversaries of their arrival in the country, citizenship ceremonies, graduations, their birthdays. There was a sense in which you created family for those whose families had been fractured or maybe decimated through war and conflict."* (Church leader, Glasgow, February 2022)

> **We heard several encouraging examples of churches and faith groups working to instil a sense of security for those placed in their locality.**

None of this is true for resettlement models that focus on hotel accommodation in arbitrarily assigned geographic communities, nor where individuals are rehoused without a say about where. We heard several encouraging examples of churches and faith groups working to instil a sense of security for those placed in their locality, particularly through sharing religious and cultural traditions as well as practical support. However, even in these cases, it was acknowledged that a model which offered secure accommodation and status from the get-go would be preferable to trying to retroactively stabilise living conditions and circumstances for vulnerable migrant families.

There is further uncertainty surrounding the Homes for Ukraine scheme, due to the fact that sponsors were required to commit to host families for a six-month period, and received financial support for that period. The first tranche of these arrangements is coming to an end, and it is projected that as many as 50,000 refugees could be left homeless.[33] This would then contribute to them experiencing housing insecurity, potentially increasing demand on both statutory and voluntary services at a time of growing general insecurity. Furthermore, this is intensified by the wider cost of living crisis because the economic position of host families has also shifted; those who six months ago felt able to host refugees in their home may now feel less able to do so due to rising household bills and grocery prices, for example.

Returning to the Old Testament framing of insecurity, verses like Deuteronomy 10:19 highlight the importance of loving and caring for those who seek refuge in a foreign country. Different translations use "resident alien", "immigrant", "foreigner", and "sojourner" to translate the Hebrew word for this category of people. While used

> **The biblical idea of a sojourner in particular conveys the instability of living temporarily in a place that is not your own.**

somewhat interchangeably depending on the translation of the Bible, the idea of the "sojourner" in particular conveys the instability of living temporarily in a place that is not your own. This is especially pertinent to the insecurity experienced by refugees and migrants in the UK today, as we have seen.

Conclusion

It is important to note that these four forms of insecurity as highlighted in our research are not discrete; for many people and communities, they intersect and lead to even more insecure or unstable circumstances. Neither are the Old Testament categories of insecurity – widows, orphans, and foreigners – entirely separate, but the emphasis is on restoring to all of them the security of belonging to a household, as it was codified in ancient Israel. Similarly, we see that the social capital and relationship offered by faith communities can go some way to mitigating some contemporary forms of insecurity and as such these are valuable community anchor points. However, as we will go on to explore in the next chapter, this is threatened when these institutions are growing more insecure and cannot guarantee their sustained presence in times of crisis. What happens when the anchors we rely on are themselves becoming looser?

1 Ipsos, *Ipsos poll shows economic optimism falls to lowest since 2008 financial crash* (2022). Available at: www.ipsos.com/en-uk/ipsos-poll-shows-economic-optimism-falls-lowest-2008-financial-crash

2 Bossert, W and C D'Ambrosio, "Measuring economic insecurity", *International Economic Review*, 54(3) (2013), pp. 1017-1030.

3 Public First, *September Polling on the Cost of Living Crisis* (2022). Available at: https://www.publicfirst.co.uk/september-polling-on-the-cost-of-living-crisis.html

4 Atchison, C J, Bowman, L, Vrinten, C, Redd, R, Pristera, P, Eaton, J W, and H. Ward, *Perceptions and behavioural responses of the general public during the COVID-19 pandemic: A cross-sectional survey of UK Adults* (2020). Available at: www.medrxiv.org/content/10.1101/2020.04.01.20050039v1

5 Jooshandeh, J, *Frontline Fatigue: Key Workers Living Through Lockdown* (London: RSA, 2020). Available at: www.thersa.org/globalassets/_foundation/new-site-blocks-and-images/reports/2020/12/frontline_fatigue.pdf

6 Ibid.

7 Pope Leo XIII, *Rerum Novarum: Encyclical Letter of Pope Leo XIII on Capital and Labour* (1891). Available at: www.vatican.va/content/leo-xiii/en/encyclicals/documents/hf_l-xiii_enc_15051891_rerum-novarum.html

8 Richardson, J, *The Living Hours Index* (2022). Available at: www.livingwage.org.uk/sites/default/files/The%20Living%20Hours%20Index%202022_0.pdf

9 Taylor, H and R Florisson, *Rise in temporary work: balancing flexibility and insecurity* (2021). Available at: www.lancaster.ac.uk/work-foundation/news/blog/rise-in-temporary-work-balancing-flexibility-and-insecurity

10 Runnymede Trust, *Ethnic inequalities in Covid-19 are playing out again – how can we stop them?* (2020). Available at: www.runnymedetrust.org/blog/ethnic-inequalities-in-covid-19-are-playing-out-again-how-can-we-stop-them

11 Muslim Council of Britain, Together in Tribulation: British Muslims and the COVID-19 Pandemic (2020). Available at: https://mcb.org.uk/wp-content/uploads/2020/11/Together-in-Tribulation-British-Muslims-and-the-COVID-19-Pandemic.pdf

12 Hunt, M, "In charts: how coronavirus is worsening Britain's racial wealth gap", the *Telegraph*, 18 June 2020. Available at: www.telegraph.co.uk/money/consumer-affairs/charts-coronavirus-worsening-britains-racial-wealth-gap/

13 Warnes, I, "10,000 Airbnbs and nowhere to live", *Open Democracy*, 2 September 2021. Available at: www.opendemocracy.net/en/opendemocracyuk/10000-airbnbs-and-nowhere-to-live-cornwalls-housing-crisis/

14 O'Shea, J, "Caught up in Cornwall's worsening housing crisis", *BBC News*, 11 May 2021. Available at: www.bbc.co.uk/news/uk-england-cornwall-61308076

15 Shelter, *Homelessness due to no-fault evictions up 37% on pre-pandemic levels* (2022). Available at: https://england.shelter.org.uk/media/press_release/homelessness_due_to_no-fault_evictions_up_37_on_pre-pandemic_levels

16 The Health Foundation, *Trends in household overcrowding by tenure* (2021). Available at: www.health.org.uk/evidence-hub/housing/housing-stability-and-security/trends-in-household-overcrowding-by-tenure

17 Wilson, W and C Barton, "Overcrowded housing (England)," *House of Commons Library Research Briefing* (2021). Available at: https://researchbriefings.files.parliament.uk/documents/SN01013/SN01013.pdf

18 National Housing Federation, *Poor housing causing health problems for nearly a third of Brits during lockdown* (2020). Available at: www.housing.org.uk/news-and-blogs/news/poor-housing-causing-health-problems-for-nearly-a-third-of-brits-during-lockdown/

19 Jones, M, "'No children, no pets, no freedom': Young renters are banned from getting on with their lives", *The i*, 17 August 2022. Available at: www.inews.co.uk/opinion/no-children-pets-freedom-young-renters-lives-1800209

20 Ministry of Housing, Communities and Local Government, *Overcrowded Housing* (2020). Available at: www.ethnicity-facts-figures.service.gov.uk/housing/housing-conditions/overcrowded-households/latest

21 Social Integration Commission, *Kingdom United? Thirteen steps to tackle social segregation* (2015). Available at: www.belongnetwork.co.uk/wp-content/uploads/2019/12/SIC-3.-Kingdom-United-Thirteen-steps-to-tackle-social-segregation.pdf

22 Butler, P, "1m UK adults 'go entire day without food' in cost of living crisis", *The Guardian*, 7 February 2022. Available at: www.theguardian.com/society/2022/feb/07/1m-uk-adults-go-entire-day-without-food-in-cost-of-living-crisis

23 Food Foundation, *Food Insecurity Tracking* (2022). Available at: https://foodfoundation.org.uk/initiatives/food-insecurity-tracking

24 Text of the speech is available at: https://churchinparliament.org/2022/10/19/archbishop-of-york-asks-whether-benefits-will-rise-with-inflation/

25 Cooper, N, Purcell, S, and R Jackson, *Below the Breadline: The Relentless Rise of Food Poverty in Britain* (2014). Available at: www.trusselltrust.org/wp-content/uploads/sites/2/2016/01/Below-the-Breadline-The-Trussell-Trust.pdf

26 Trussell Trust, *End of Year Stats*, 2021-22 (2022). Available at: www.trusselltrust.org/news-and-blog/latest-stats/end-year-stats/

27 Church Urban Fund, *Church in Action Report 2015* (2015). Available at: www.hrballiance.org.uk/wp-content/uploads/2018/12/Church-in-Action-2015_0.pdf

28 Church Urban Fund, Church in Action Report 2020/21 (2021). Available at: https://cuf.org.uk/uploads/resources/Church-In-Action-Report.pdf

29 Magic Breakfast, *Magic Breakfast Partner School Survey 2022: Our year in numbers* (2022). Available at: www.magicbreakfast.com/blog/magic-breakfast-partner-school-survey-2022-our-year-in-numbers

30 IPPR, *Revealed: Working family poverty hits record high, fuelled by rising housing costs and childcare challenges* (2021). Available at: www.ippr.org/news-and-media/press-releases/revealed-working-family-poverty-hits-record-high-fuelled-by-rising-housing-costs-and-childcare-challenges

31 Sharma, S. "'Heartbreakingly ironic': Outrage over food banks closing for Queen's funeral", *The Independent*, 14 September 2022. Available at: www.independent.co.uk/news/uk/home-news/food-banks-uk-close-queen-elizabeth-funeral-b2166769.html

32 Taylor, D, "Use of UK hotels for asylum seekers trebles despite Home Office promise", *The Guardian*, 21 July 2022. Available at: www.theguardian.com/politics/2022/jul/21/use-of-uk-hotels-for-asylum-seekers-trebles-despite-home-office-promise

33 Bryant, M and M Townsend, "50,000 Ukrainian refugees in UK facing homelessness 'disaster' next year", *The Guardian*, 28 August 2022. Available at: www.theguardian.com/world/2022/aug/28/50000-ukrainian-refugees-in-uk-facing-homelessness-disaster-next-year-homes-for-ukraine

A social recession

Having observed how the communities in our research describe the individual and household effects of insecurity, we now turn to what this might mean for community groups and civil society. In the aftermath of the 2008 financial crisis, researchers at LSE suggested that the UK experienced a "social recession" alongside the economic one.[1] An economic recession is a contraction in the economy which leads to a general decline in economic activity. A social recession, therefore, might similarly be defined as a general decline in voluntary and community activity, in terms of both time and financial resources, in response to the effects of an economic event. While it is too soon to know for certain whether this will be the case with the current crisis, the idea of a social recession is a helpful way of viewing the effects on the charitable sector of both the pandemic and current economic crisis. These effects are already being seen and articulated by research participants. We argue that we are now seeing a significant social recession emerging.

Volunteering capacity

Statistics showed that formal volunteering declined by 6% between 2008 and 2011, reaching the lowest levels for a decade and contributing to the social recession first described by LSE researchers. Levels of informal volunteering also fell by 12%, representing the "kind of decline normally seen over decades and between generations" rather than over the course of just two years.[2] Researchers found that controlling for individual economic hardship did not sufficiently explain this civic

> **The gap in rates of formal volunteering between the most and least disadvantaged communities has widened.**

withdrawal, but that the level of deprivation in a community was a greater factor. The gap in rates of formal volunteering between the most and least disadvantaged communities widened, and similar gaps in informal volunteering emerged where they had not previously been observed. Regions with higher levels of unemployment during the crisis also saw a sharper decline in both formal and informal volunteering.[3]

There are two opposing hypotheses for patterns of civic engagement during a crisis: the mobilisation hypothesis, which suggests that crises might lead to greater civic engagement because of the rallying effect; and the retreat hypothesis, which asserts that as people's resources are stretched, their capacity for voluntary action is reduced. A cross-national study of voluntary association membership after the 2008 crisis found that data supported the retreat hypothesis, with no evidence of mobilisation especially among those most susceptible to the economic effects of the crisis.[4] Membership declined overall, with countries harder hit by the crisis more likely to experience such declines. The profile of those engaged in voluntary associations was similar before and after the crisis, with those in better-off and more secure economic groups more likely to be active.

It remains to be seen whether these patterns will be replicated during and after the current economic crisis, especially coming so soon after the COVID-19 pandemic, which itself had a significant impact on volunteering. There was something of a boom in informal volunteering in the early days of the pandemic, with the advent of local mutual aid groups and community support favouring the mobilisation hypothesis. Levels of informal volunteering rose by 2% in 2020-21, with the furlough scheme seen to lead to an increase in working-age people volunteering in their communities. The NHS volunteer recruitment drive attracted numbers of volunteers not seen since the Second World War, although this was not always effectively deployed.[5] On the other hand, formal volunteering, which had remained stable since 2015 after recovering slightly from 2011 levels, fell by a fifth.[6] Some of this might be attributed to the fact that many formal volunteering projects were forced to shut their doors due to public health restrictions, and community efforts were therefore channelled into informal means of support.

Many of the organisations in our research noted that, while they had benefited from the aforementioned boom in volunteering because of furlough, they had also seen a number of their existing volunteers withdraw from involvement, especially some of their longstanding supporters. This was largely due to them being on average older and therefore more likely to be shielding or isolating themselves for health reasons. This economic crisis therefore represents a double challenge to groups already trying to rebuild their resources:

> **Many of the organisations in our research noted that they had also seen a number of their existing volunteers withdraw from involvement.**

"We've seen a lot of longstanding volunteers step back. A few people have decided to move into different roles, but even before the demand for what we do went up, more people have just decided not to take stuff back up post-Covid. How we resource our community outreach from a human perspective will be a lot more challenging." (Church leader, Wolverhampton, May 2022)

For faith communities, this was true both in terms of volunteering at social action projects and also in terms of contributing to worship; for example, several church communities reported having fewer people on the reading rota now. There are also practical implications where voluntary groups or services evolved during the pandemic but now find themselves having to adapt to post-pandemic circumstances. The coordinator of a food bank in Glasgow told us how they had come to rely on local supermarkets offering them surplus food at the end of the day, but that this was dependent on someone being able to collect it at 8pm. During the pandemic, she said that people were more willing to go out in the evening and fulfil this role but that the majority of their volunteers had now returned to their 9-5 jobs and were less able to facilitate this collection after a full day at work:

> *"There is an increase in demand for food, obviously, but trying to find a way to collect it and get it to people is difficult when volunteers are stretched. As people have been going back to work, it's harder to find anyone who can go and pick up the food at 8pm or 9pm."* (Food bank coordinator, Glasgow, May 2022)

This is intensified by the rise in petrol prices making it more expensive for these volunteers to drive to collect food. In many cases, we found that withdrawal from volunteering was due to an inability to afford it now, rather than the lack of willingness to do so.

In the way it stimulated volunteering among the temporarily unemployed, the furlough scheme is an interesting case study. It offered a degree of security which is not typically afforded to those unemployed due to crises. We argue that this stability, albeit in the short term, was critical to the high levels of civic mobilisation seen in the early days of the pandemic.

In other words, government interventions to ensure financial stability during crises can enable individuals to contribute to their community and engage in civil society, without worrying about their uncertain income. The way welfare provision is designed can thus stimulate volunteering capacity.

The furlough payments were also offered with relatively few strings attached on behalf of the recipient, unlike other mechanisms of the welfare state. We heard several examples of voluntary and faith groups whose work is sustained by those with no right to work because of their migration status. The particular sort of insecurity experienced by refugees or asylum seekers who cannot legally work means that there are fewer outlets for them to contribute to community life and take on positions of civic responsibility which would afford them dignity.

Faith communities and voluntary groups are one such outlet. However, the constraints of government structures make this difficult; one charity worker spoke about the challenges of volunteers who needed to report regularly to the Home Office or to the job centre, but do not always know exactly when. They are keen to volunteer but due to matters beyond their control, cannot always do so with enough regularity. Where appropriate, a degree of informality around volunteering commitments, with necessary safeguards, can facilitate this; for example, staff at a soup kitchen spoke about not requiring volunteers to sign up on a formal system. This arose from recognising the unclear immigration status of some of those in the community, which would render it inappropriate to keep lists of their names and details without good reason.

In particular for smaller organisations, there is a reluctance to turn down anyone who is eager to volunteer, but this must be balanced against the increased uncertainty that comes with some volunteer demographics, whether because of their migration status, employment patterns, or economic position. We heard examples of individuals establishing themselves in volunteer roles, only to be resettled to another borough or even another area of the country at the whim of the authorities and with little notice. This is destabilising for all involved.

Occasionally, however, this can offer an opportunity for voluntary groups, which become a source of hope and purpose for people. The volunteer coordinator of a social integration project in Newham told the story of an individual who had seen volunteering as a way of finding meaning in uncertain circumstances linked to being rehoused across the city from where her children were in school. Initially, she was looking for somewhere to sit during the day, between dropping off and picking her children up, because it was neither feasible nor affordable for her to travel home and back again. She began volunteering at the community centre as a means of doing something profitable in that time.

> **Community groups are often reliant on volunteers who have relatively insecure lives.**

Yet this highlights again how reliant community groups often are on volunteers who have relatively insecure lives and circumstances themselves. We heard from one core volunteer who is the mainstay of a local Islamic charity and also of the local mosque, while working two jobs and having significant family responsibilities. They acknowledged that, if they were not able to attend mosque or fulfil a volunteer shift, even on one particular day, their absence would be felt and the community would be affected, but their circumstances often made this inevitable. Some voluntary positions are more accessible to people in uncertain circumstances than others; there is a need for those who are able to commit long term and strategically, as well as those who can fill the gaps.

Financial giving

When individuals and households are struggling economically, it is somewhat inevitable that the community collectively begins to experience the effects. As this spreads, the whole voluntary sector experiences the impact of growing economic instability, as became increasingly apparent over the course of our research as energy bills rose. A survey of charity leaders by Charities Aid Foundation (CAF) in May 2022 found that a third feared their charities would struggle to survive as a result of the crisis. Of those surveyed, 60% were worried that people would have less money to donate to charity, and 70% were concerned about a rising demand for services.[7]

Squeezed personal finances and rising organisational overheads at a time when funders are also tightening their purse strings makes for a perfect storm for charities and community groups.

> **Squeezed personal finances and rising organisational overheads at a time when funders are also tightening their purse strings makes for a perfect storm for charities and community groups.**

"In the early days of lockdown, people were very generous. I think they all raided their piggy banks then and probably haven't got

anything left!" (Hostel manager, Wolverhampton, April 2022)

With volunteers, we saw how the pandemic sparked an initial mobilisation of informal support, followed by a retreat. Discussing the situation regarding funding for charity and community work, several interviewees suggested that the same pattern was reflected by grant makers and funders and, in many cases, individual donors. Back in spring 2020, few factored into their funding calculations quite how long the COVID-19 pandemic would last, nor could have foreseen the other ensuing factors that have led to the current cost of living crisis. As a result, some funders over-committed in the early days of the pandemic and now have restricted resources left.

According to CAF data, there were above average levels of charitable giving in the early phase of the first lockdown in spring 2020, followed by a significant decline later in the year without the usual rise in giving at Christmas. Individual donation levels remained lower than average throughout 2021.[8]

A community development worker echoed this, talking about grant-making organisations:

"A lot of them front-loaded stuff because there was a big push around the initial year of the pandemic. You had that huge push then, but no one was expecting it to go on this long, and you then get a pull back. Lots of stuff was funded then but they haven't got as much to dish out now so you end up with a constricted pot of funds available for the rebuilding work. A lot of charitable trusts over-committed in the first year and are now having to withdraw." (Community development worker, Wolverhampton, February 2022)

The language of "rebuilding" in this conversation suggests the belief – shared by some of our earlier interviewees – that as the pandemic receded, the time was ripe for reconstructing and renewing some of the social infrastructure damaged by it, and healing the economic scars left behind. Yet just ten days after this particular interview took place, Russia invaded Ukraine and the ramifications for the economy became apparent. Rather than rebuilding, we are instead facing the further disintegration of our safety net, with funding streams similarly weakened.

The pandemic changed patterns of giving to charity, for both economic and practical reasons. One Muslim community leader talked about how the enforced absence of Friday prayers during the pandemic had had a lasting impact on the finances of many local mosques, which had typically relied on cash donations. Up to 75% of annual income for some mosques comes through cash giving.[9] Without the focal point of Friday prayers, nor physical gatherings during Ramadan in 2020, it was not possible to collect money physically and not all worshippers transitioned to other forms of giving.

This was also observed in other faith groups; in the Church of England, giving via physical collections in church fell by half from 2019 to 2020.[10] Across the charity sector as a whole, cash giving fell substantially during the pandemic, with only 9% of people saying they had done so in May and June 2020, compared with 51% the previous year, and this remained subdued by mid-2021.[11]

It was noted by participants that this had a more pronounced impact on the most precarious congregations, not only in the Muslim community, because people whose incomes are insecure or vary month to month are not always able to set up direct debits or regular giving, but are often very generous with cash in times when they have the means. In the Church of England, average income across all parishes fell between 2019 and 2020, but parishes with higher income to begin with generally saw a lower reduction in percentage terms.[12]

The community energy crisis

Against this backdrop of tightened budgets and shrinking income, a key concern for many of the communities we heard from was the rise in energy bills. Spaces like community centres, church buildings, Scout huts, and other hubs of community activity are subject to business rates for utilities and, unlike domestic rates, these are not capped. For those not on fixed-term deals, there was therefore no limit to how much these bills will rise by this winter, nor any easy way of forecasting it.

In every sector of the community, from village halls[13] to pubs[14] and even schools[15], there has been concern about what this will mean. The average energy bill in 2019 for Church of England churches located in "estate parishes" – classed as those with 500+ social housing homes – represented 6% of their recurring income. If uncapped energy bills for these churches rose equivalent to commercial prices, then by winter, it was forecast that this figure could be as high as a quarter of their recurring income.[16] This is only one subset of one church denomination, but it indicates the likely impact on the finances of congregations and groups in the areas least equipped to deal with them and the communities

> **In every sector of the community, from village halls to pubs and even schools, there has been concern about what rising energy bills will will mean.**

with the narrowest economic margins to begin with. A large mosque in Birmingham reported being told that its energy bills could quadruple from £60,000 to £250,000 a year and was considering cutting back on community activity significantly as a result.[17] Churches of various denominations report being given similar quotes from energy brokers.[18]

When the dire household-level implications of the energy crisis began to emerge, there were suggestions from many that churches and similar buildings might operate as "warm banks" to offer warmth and welcome to those who could not afford to heat their homes during the winter months. In early March 2022, one church leader in the most deprived part of Glasgow described how the number of pastoral home visits he was asked to make had dwindled. He had realised this was because people were already struggling to heat their homes but were ashamed of others knowing this. The solution he proposed was to invite them for a cup of coffee in the church building, or in a local supermarket café instead, both institutions which at that stage seemed large and resilient enough to absorb the energy costs and keep the heating on. However, the scale of the situation subsequently progressed to a point where this could not be assumed.

> **Without concerted action to address these rising bills, the longevity and financial sustainability of the buildings themselves will be threatened.**

Without concerted action to address these rising bills, the longevity and financial sustainability of the buildings themselves will be threatened, and it is not only faith institutions which will be at risk of being lost as a result. It was welcome, therefore, that in mid-September 2022, the then Prime Minister Liz Truss announced a package of measures including a price guarantee for businesses and third sector buildings, including places of worship. This will restrict energy bills for these spaces for six months. Wholesale rates this winter are expected to be £600 per megawatt hour (MWh) for electricity and £180/MWh for mains gas. The government's price guarantee for non-domestic customers restricts this to £211/MWh for electricity and £75/MWh for gas.[19] This represents a reduction of 65% and 58% respectively on the projected cost per unit, which is a welcome intervention although still significantly higher than the annual bills these churches were used to. In addition, the Church Commissioners recently announced a £15 million package of help for Church of England churches and clergy struggling to pay their energy bills.[20]

> **More action is needed to stabilise these energy costs over the longer term, not just the next six months.**

More action is needed, however, to stabilise these costs over the longer term, not just the next six months. Otherwise, there is a distinct possibility that some will still shut due to the cost of heating their buildings, even in communities where there is a thriving and active congregation.

"When the bills keep going up, our Scout group simply won't survive that. We've had the building for years, but the rates are going up too much." (Scout leader, Newham, August 2022)

Prior to the emergence of the energy crisis, the cost of maintaining physical spaces was already a significant challenge. For organisations and projects which do not own a building, the finances and logistics of renting them was also a substantial issue.

The coordinator of a soup kitchen providing meals to people in Wolverhampton spoke about the growing problem of finding affordable premises to operate from, having had to leave two different venues in the course of the pandemic. The project was initially based in the building of a church which subsequently shut, then was helped by a local café which then closed down too. Local churches have increased the fees they charge to rent the space, out of necessity, and this has priced out some of the very community organisations they typically host.

"The church used to cost a fiver a session. Now we're looking around for somewhere similar and it's about £50 an hour or something crazy. Even church buildings are out of our league."
(Soup kitchen coordinator, Wolverhampton, May 2022)

The lack of physical premises, or the stability of a permanent place to operate from, can also represent a challenge in seeking funding, as the same interviewee went on to describe:

"It's that thing that if you're homeless, you can't get a bank account, but if you can't get a job, you can't get a home. It's the same for us as a project, really. I haven't got premises so when I ask for funding, I can't give people a registered address, which makes it difficult."

Some of these community groups have relied on the generosity of churches and other buildings charging a minimal amount for the use of the building. One church leader talked about how their congregation had not charged any rent to community groups using their community centre since the beginning of the pandemic, choosing to subsidise it as part of their collective generosity. This had allowed valuable community groups to continue running, as well as offering free workspace to local people wanting to gain employment or start small businesses. This had been "a real privilege" for the church to be able to offer, but the energy crisis threatened to end the arrangement, he said.

All of this applies equally to many non-faith-based community buildings too. Like church halls, none of these can put their rent up proportionately to the amount by which their utility bills are rising.

If the price of renting a church hall or similar space was increased by the same degree that wholesale gas has increased by in the last 12 months, and this increase was passed on to families coming to a parent and toddler group, they might be charged up to £15 per session. This would quickly undermine their purpose as affordable community activities. This is all before the effects of inflation on the cost of buying refreshments like orange squash (up 7% this year according to the Office of National Statistics (ONS)) and biscuits (up 35%) is taken into account, as we will go on to see.[21]

This underlines how critical these community spaces are and how vital it is that they are sustained beyond this economic crisis. As several participants noted, the activities hosted there play an important social role as well as material support. There are early indications that the cost of living crisis is contributing to increasing loneliness as people withdraw from spending money on socialising,[22] and pubs are threatened with closure, all of which would be compounded by the absence of free spaces for social interaction in the community.

> **There are early indications that the cost of living crisis is contributing to increasing loneliness.**

The impact of rising fuel costs

The rising price of petrol was one of the first indicators of inflation, noticeable in everyday life even before the scale of the energy crisis was evident. The price of filling a car at the fuel pumps has climbed consistently since the beginning of 2022, reaching a record high in June.[23] As early as March, we heard concerns from community groups across the country about the impact of rising fuel costs on the aspects of their work that relied on private transport. This has had a significant impact on their volunteers and their capacity to operate projects like food deliveries to vulnerable people.

> **Rising petrol costs significant impact on community capacity to operate projects like food deliveries to vulnerable people.**

Some models of community action rely on the implicit assumption that volunteers will also have the means to contribute financially to the work of the organisation. One project coordinator in the West Midlands told us they relied on their retired volunteers using their own cars to operate the delivery service, and that these volunteers had historically absorbed their own fuel costs or considered it part of their financial giving. However, this could no longer be taken for granted, we heard, because of rising fuel costs.

"During Covid especially, there was a real need for drivers. Now we're finding that fuel costs are a challenge. Whether volunteers can afford to continue driving their cars around the city delivering food is a real concern... There's also a value to having something local that people can get to without having to pay for public transport." (Charity worker, Glasgow, March 2022)

Another volunteer in East London told us towards the beginning of the research that he donated the equivalent of £50 a week to the church, through the cost of running his own car; by the end of the research, the same volunteer had assessed his own personal finances and made the difficult decision to stop supporting the service in order to save money. Even if he could still have afforded a weekly £50, that sum would now only cover a fraction of the deliveries it previously had.

The cost of petrol has risen by over 60% in the last 12 months, although it is falling again at the time of writing.[24] At its peak, this effectively meant either that each food delivery cost 60% more, or that volunteers could carry out fewer deliveries for the same amount of money.

There is a government scheme – the Approved Mileage Allowance Payment – which controls the level of travel expenses that volunteer drivers can be reimbursed for without it affecting their tax obligations or benefit entitlement. There have been calls from the charity sector for the rate at which this is paid to be raised in recognition of the rising cost of fuel. A coalition of charities affected by this issue stated in July 2022 that the current rate "no longer fully covers volunteer expenses" and they were concerned it would disincentivise volunteering in the face of the cost of living crisis.[25]

However, a rise in reimbursement presupposes that community groups have the financial reserves to pay this, and it did not appear from our research that many local churches and faith groups paid this sort of expense anyway. For some, this raised questions about what it meant to give generously, even at personal cost. Several volunteers told us that, in better economic circumstances, they would not have felt comfortable taking petrol money from the church for activities they felt were part of practising their faith. Whether they used the language of "Christian giving" or the Muslim "sadaqa", people of various different faiths talked about how they had seen paying for petrol as part of their religiously motivated charity and therefore taking expenses would detract from this.

"Having worked in other charities, I think it's always good practice to offer travel expenses to volunteers. It feels a bit different managing volunteers who are part of a church as opposed to volunteers more generally though, because for some people they feel that's part of their giving to the church. It has a different feeling to it, but you don't want anyone to be excluded from giving their time on grounds of income." (Volunteer coordinator, March 2022, Glasgow)

One non-faith-based organisation had made the decision to fund transport for volunteers where required, usually up to £4.50 a shift, in order to facilitate people coming, but did not have the capacity to fund this for all volunteers. Another charity manager talked about the difficulty of ensuring that their longstanding volunteers were able to continue participating if they wanted to, while not wanting to embarrass them by offering to pay for a bus fare to facilitate this. This was intensified by the fact that, as social housing tenants, some of the volunteers had been moved to houses further away from the neighbourhood without having any agency in this decision.

The "custard cream conundrum"

The perfect storm of the pandemic and the economic crisis has revealed the precariousness not only of individual lives but also of many of the structures that have long sustained the voluntary and faith sectors. We call this the "custard cream conundrum". In the same way that people using their own cars and quietly donating fuel has sustained many delivery services, many projects like toddler groups have been sustained by volunteers paying for refreshments out of their own pockets. If the cost of this has been absorbed by the generosity of volunteers until now, it is a considerable expense that churches may not have budgeted for. If budgets are tightened, however, people may find they can no longer manage this, or else the volunteer who has been subsidising it may have left.

> **The perfect storm of the pandemic and the economic crisis has revealed the precariousness of the structures that sustain the voluntary and faith sectors.**

It may seem like a trivial example; after all, a 200g packet of own-brand custard cream biscuits only costs 21p.[26] However, it all adds up. If every parish church consumed one packet of biscuits a week, this would amount to a combined total of £131,040 a year in the Church of England alone. If every parish wanted chocolate bourbon creams instead (26p for 200g), that would amount to an extra £31,200 a year. One packet of custard creams a week is a conservative estimate, even before considering other denominations and groups; if each church got through two packets of biscuits, that would cost the Church of England over £250,000 a year. As we will go on to explore, inflation is also a significant concern here. If the price of biscuits went up by 5%, or roughly 2p per packet, this would be an additional £12,500 a year for the Church to either cover or to fundraise from volunteers – a sum which no longer seems quite so trivial. At the level of the local church, the figures are smaller but still reflect additional costs and margins than have not previously been accounted for, at a time when resources are tighter than ever.

A similar example of resources that are not formally designated but quietly sustained is the informal institutional knowledge held by individuals without it ever being part of their job description. The margins of community groups are often small enough that one individual volunteer is the difference between a project functioning and not. As one lay church leader reflected in May 2022:

> **The margins of community groups are often small enough that one individual volunteer is the difference between a project functioning and not.**

"It's the fragility and precariousness of the whole structure. It takes one dedicated volunteer to stop what they're doing, to be priced out of what they're doing, for that whole important service to the community to be lost... The precarious economic climate actually highlights how precarious the systems of the church are themselves.

Whether there is economic instability or not, the church should not be reliant on one main volunteer. It's like the economic instability highlights that and what the problems are, a bit like how Covid shed light on inequalities we all knew were there but didn't highlight. It's shedding light on pre-existing problems within that community." (Lay leader, East London, June 2022)

We heard how in many communities and organisations, administrative staff are well placed to know which families are struggling or in need of support, without it being acknowledged as part of their role. A school secretary, for example, might have the financial management of dinner money as part of their job description, through which they gain insight into which families are experiencing insecurity and might exercise some flexibility in managing this. If this individual moves on, this role might not be officially handed over, with consequences for the families as well as school finances. The same might be true of those charged with administrative responsibility in faith communities.

Just as it is not written down formally that the cost of biscuits is absorbed by volunteers, the social stability offered by these individuals is vital but not noticed formally until it is no longer offered.

The impact of inflation

The effects of inflation, felt keenly at the supermarket checkout, are also reaching community groups and faith institutions, with severe implications for their work. Some of the most valuable community activities in social terms are also the most costly in terms of the energy they require and therefore how much they are affected by inflation, particularly those centred on food.

Take, for example, a church lunch club for the elderly, which offers a hot meal, warm room, and friendly company for its weekly guests. According to the most recently available ONS data from October 2022, the cost of dried pasta has risen by 60%, tomatoes by 19% and cheese by 10%, although the price of minced beef has fallen slightly by 7%, collectively making a basic pot of spaghetti Bolognese a considerably more expensive option than a year ago.[27] The price of teabags has risen by 46% and instant coffee by 19%, which further contributes to the higher grocery bill for the lunch club kitchen. Add to this the cost of heating the hall, using the gas hob to cook the meal, and keeping the fridge running, along with the increased petrol costs of a volunteer driving to the supermarket to buy ingredients, and the scale of the problem becomes starker. The £3 that guests might contribute each week suddenly won't stretch as far. Not all lunch club guests come because they are materially struggling; many come for the company, but they too will suffer if these spaces are forced to shut.

There are similar resourcing challenges for community social activities and food banks, which both rely on the generosity of individuals donating food, whether for food parcels or for refreshments at coffee mornings or lunch clubs. We heard fears that the rising price of groceries together with restricted household incomes will have an impact on donations. The Food Foundation has tracked the total price of a basket of basic grocery items since April 2022. It finds that it has increased by over 8% and inflation has not yet finished rising.[28] If people are paying this much more for their weekly shop, their capacity to add items to donate may be restricted. A food bank in Scotland reported recently that the cost of a food parcel had risen by as much as £19.[29]

These sorts of calculations – the cost of a tin of beans, a full tank of petrol, or the ability to donate refreshments for a church coffee morning from your own pocket without claiming the money back – are the small margins on which whole communities have relied, but which are dwindling further. If marginal gains are the small, incremental improvements which collectively make a significant improvement for a business, we might conversely describe the unexpected cost of a packet of custard creams or a tank of petrol as "marginal losses" for charities and community groups.

Modelling by researchers at Pro Bono Economics emphasises this. For the past five years the median average donation made in the UK has been roughly £20 a month, with few charities seeing average donations rise with inflation even before this crisis.[30] Using the Bank of England's most recent inflation forecasts, Pro Bono Economics projects that this £20 in 2017 will be worth just £15.30 in 2023 and £14.90 in 2024.[31] Total charitable donations in the first half of this year were worth £5.7 billion and based on this, by the end of the year that sum will be worth £5.2 billion because of inflation. There are behavioural challenges here; committing to give a round number like £20 (or £10) is a comfortable habit because even when paid by direct debit, it is easy to conceive of in terms of a currency note. However, this poses a challenge to charities who have not seen their giving increase in line with inflation, at the same time that the cost of services and staffing is rising.

There is an encouragement to charities here, however. One charitable giving platform we heard from has seen 90% of its regular givers increase their donations in line with inflation annually. The platform, which facilitates giving to local churches, attributes this to the fact that when a giver renews their monthly donation for another year, they are actively asked if they would like to increase this in line with that year's inflation index. Even those giving comparatively small regular donations are more likely than not to opt into this. The challenge to other charities is therefore to give their regular direct debit givers this option too, in order to mitigate some of the effects of inflation on the value of giving, even if charitable giving still falls overall because of the cost of living.

> We argue that there is also a risk that this will lead to "social scarring".

Social scarring

The combined impact of all these factors, from the cost of energy to the impact of successive crises on volunteering and giving habits, constitutes the possibility of a "social recession". This being the case, we argue that there is also a risk that this will lead to "social scarring". Economic scarring refers to the medium to long-term impacts of economic crises, which endure in communities long after the economy is seen to have recovered or bounced back. Even once economic indicators suggest that the shock of a recession has been weathered, its effects on community and individual financial circumstances are not instantly reversed. This economic scarring lingers and has a cost.

Similarly, if there is a social recession in tandem with the economic one, its effects will also linger, constituting social scarring. Community cohesion, relationships, and lost spiritual practices, for example, are difficult to rebuild. Even if the housing market were to become more affordable, or second home ownership was outlawed, families and young people who have moved away from an area because of it would not automatically return if they have since built a life for themselves elsewhere. Nor would the structures of communities instantaneously be reconstructed. One older church member acknowledged that while they had for a time maintained a Sunday school for only two or three children, the critical mass of both volunteers and children needed to re-establish one would probably be higher. The scarring effect of the pandemic is also evident in the numbers of volunteers and worshippers who have not returned to their previous habits and practices, even once the public health emergency subsided.

1. Lim, C and Laurence, J, "Doing good when times are bad", *The British Journal of Sociology*, 66 (2015), pp. 319–344. Available at: https://doi.org/10.1111/1468-4446.12122

2. Laurence, J, "The UK experienced a sharp drop in volunteering behaviour following the Great Recession", *LSE Politics and Policy* (2015). Available at: https://blogs.lse.ac.uk/politicsandpolicy/drop-in-volunteering-post-recession/

3. Lim and Laurence, "Doing good when times are bad".

4. Cameron, S, "Civic engagement in times of economic crisis: A cross-national comparative study of voluntary association membership", *European Political Science Review*, 13(3) (2021), pp. 265–283. Available at: https://doi.org/10.1017/S1755773921000060

5. Butler, P, "A million volunteer to help NHS and others during Covid-19 outbreak", *The Guardian*, 13 April 2022. Available at: www.theguardian.com/society/2020/apr/13/a-million-volunteer-to-help-nhs-and-others-during-covid-19-lockdown

6. NCVO, *Civil Society Almanac: Volunteering* (2021). Available at: www.ncvo.org.uk/news-and-insights/news-index/uk-civil-society-almanac-2021/volunteering/#/

7. Hargrave, R, "A third of charities fear for their survival because of cost-of-living crisis, survey finds", *Third Sector* (2022). Available at: www.thirdsector.co.uk/third-charities-fear-survival-cost-of-living-crisis-survey-finds/management/article/1754670

8. Charities Aid Foundation, *UK Giving Report 2021* (2021). Available at: www.cafonline.org/docs/default-source/about-us-research/uk_giving_report_2021.pdf

9. Muslim Council of Britain, *Together in Tribulation: British Muslims and the COVID-19 Pandemic* (2020). Available at: https://mcb.org.uk/wp-content/uploads/2020/11/Together-in-Tribulation-British-Muslims-and-the-COVID-19-Pandemic.pdf

10. Church of England Research and Statistics, *Parish Finance Statistics* (2020). Available at: www.churchofengland.org/sites/default/files/2022-02/Parish%20Finance%20Statistics%202020.pdf

11. Ferrell-Schweppenstedde, D, "How has the pandemic impacted our behaviours in giving to charity?" *Charities Aid Foundation* (2021). Available at: www.cafonline.org/about-us/blog-home/how-has-the-pandemic-impacted-our-behaviours-in-giving-to-charity

12. Church of England Research and Statistics, *Parish Finance Statistics*.

13 Action with Communities in Rural England (ACRE), *England's village halls asked about the impact of rising energy prices* (2022). Available at: https://acre.org.uk/press-release-englands-village-halls-asked-about-the-impact-of-rising-energy-prices/

14 Davies, R, "Thousands of UK pubs 'face closure' without energy bills support", *The Guardian*, 30 August 2022. Available at: www.theguardian.com/business/2022/aug/30/thousands-of-uk-pubs-face-closure-without-energy-bills-support

15 Belger, T, "'Apocalyptic': 500 per cent energy price hikes plunge schools into winter crisis", *Schools Week*, 6 September 2022. Available at: www.schoolsweek.co.uk/school-energy-bills-government-help-apocalyptic-rises

16 Figures from Dave Champness on Twitter.

17 Birmingham Mail, *Green Lane Mosque "could partially close" amid £250k energy quote shock* (2022). Available at: www.birminghammail.co.uk/news/midlands-news/green-lane-mosque-could-partially-24950190

18 Paveley, R, "Parishes feel the squeeze as energy bills rocket", *Church Times*, 19 August 2022. Available at: www.churchtimes.co.uk/articles/2022/19-august/news/uk/parishes-feel-the-squeeze-as-energy-bills-rocket

19 Department for Business, Energy and Industrial Strategy, *Energy bills support factsheet* (2022). Available at: www.gov.uk/government/publications/energy-bills-support/energy-bills-support-factsheet-8-september-2022#support-for-businesses-and-non-domestic-properties

20 Ashworth, P, "Commissioners offer £15 million to help parishes and clergy meet energy costs", *Church Times*, 14 October 2022. Available at: www.churchtimes.co.uk/articles/2022/14-october/news/uk/commissioners-offer-15-million-to-help-parishes-and-clergy-meet-energy-costs

21 Office of National Statistics data (2022). Available at: www.ons.gov.uk/economy/inflationandpriceindices/articles/trackingthelowestcostgroceryitemsukexperimentalanalysis/april2021toseptember2022

22 Skopeliti, C, "'It's become lonelier': Britons cut back on socialising as cost of living soars", *The Guardian*, 24 August 2022. Available at: www.theguardian.com/business/2022/aug/24/its-become-lonelier-britons-cut-back-on-socialising-as-cost-of-living-soars

23 Boyle, C, "Petrol prices fall from record highs for first time in months", *The Guardian*, 18 July 2022. Available at: www.theguardian.com/uk-news/2022/jul/18/petrol-prices-fall-from-record-highs-for-first-time-in-months

24 Based on RAC data available here: www.racfoundation.org/data/uk-pump-prices-over-time

25 Community Transport Association, *Charities call on chancellor to tackle fuel costs crisis* (2022). Available at: https://ctauk.org/charities-call-on-chancellor-to-tackle-fuel-costs-crisis/

26 Price from Aldi website, 1 October 2022.

27 ONS data.

28 Food Foundation, *Food Prices Tracking: August Update* (2022). Available at: https://foodfoundation.org.uk/news/food-prices-tracking-august-update

29 BBC News, *Contents of a single parcel go up by £19 - food bank provider*, 26 October 2022. Available at: www.bbc.co.uk/news/uk-scotland-63385874

30 Charities Aid Foundation, *UK Giving Report 2022* (2022). Available at: www.cafonline.org/docs/default-source/about-us-research/uk_giving_2022.pdf

31 O'Halloran, J and N Sykes, "The cost of giving: What UK charities need to know about inflation", *Pro Bono Economics* (2022). Available at: www.probonoeconomics.com/Handlers/Download.ashx?IDMF=ec350d40-d510-4e0c-883c-9e84be2b9020

Recommendations

As observed throughout the research, insecurity in its various forms is a structural and engrained problem experienced by communities across the country, from housing to employment, access to food to migration status. It is a fundamentally social and relational problem; what might begin as economic insecurity leads to weakened social ties and affects the cohesion of entire communities. Further, we have seen how this instability is spreading to the entire faith and voluntary sector, as the cost of living crisis rages and institutions that act as anchors to whole communities become untethered as a result of what we argue is an emerging social recession. The safety net of charities and community groups which offer security to those in precarious circumstances is now at risk. If the effects of this are not addressed effectively, it is possible that valuable institutions like churches may shut, leaving economic and social scars on the community.

> **The safety net of charities and community groups which offer security to those in precarious circumstances is now at risk.**

We therefore propose solutions that address structural insecurity, for individuals and households as well as for communities and institutions. These recommendations are aimed at sustaining community groups and institutions like churches and charities, both in terms of the invaluable human capital they hold and the physical spaces their buildings represent, so that they are able to continue supporting individuals in a period of growing economic insecurity nationally.

As we identify throughout the research, there are longer-term forms of insecurity, which predate the current crisis and for which longer-term solutions are required. This is especially true of housing insecurity. We suggest that it could be **made easier for local communities and faith groups to invest in assets like housing for local residents.** The Charities Act 2011 requires charitable organisations selling land or property to achieve the best possible price for it, unless there are compelling reasons otherwise.[1] In practice, this means charities and churches are often forced to sell to corporate developers, and the resulting properties are unaffordable for local community members. We heard multiple examples of churches that had wanted to sell off land for social purposes, such as much-needed affordable housing for local people, but were constrained by this legislation and therefore sold to private developers instead. Relaxing or amending this legislation, or making it easier for compelling reasons to be argued, would be beneficial for the whole community.

Churches and faith groups could also explore **alternative models of housing** in an effort to make sure that homes in their local area remain genuinely affordable. One such model is that of Community Land Trusts, of which there are now over 500 in England and Wales.[2] These ensure that land and assets remain in trust, and are sold and resold at rates pegged to local income. They are also democratic organisations run by local people, including people of faith in numerous examples, which build social capital at the same time as increasing housing security. The same model has also been used to secure community assets such as post offices, libraries, and shops, allowing local people to come together and buy local institutions that would otherwise have closed. We recommend

greater faith-based involvement in these models of community security.

For volunteers, we note that the flexibility and financial security offered by the furlough scheme was hugely valuable in supporting people to contribute in their local community, in ways that have not all been sustained beyond the furlough period. We argue that there are measures that could give employees the flexibility to continue contributing in this way, for example **a four-day week, greater employer support for paid volunteering leave, or a tax break for volunteering time**. All these would require rethinking how we value paid work alongside unpaid community work, shaking up employment patterns to allow people to combine both while still enjoying a secure financial position and regular income where possible. This would in turn allow charities and faith groups to draw on a larger pool of potential volunteers rather than relying too heavily on retirees or those with lots of free time during the working week. Changes in the tax code for paying petrol and other expenses to volunteers could also incentivise this further.

In terms of funding, we suggest that **raising the rate of Gift Aid** on charitable donations would benefit charities and faith groups. At present, charities can claim an extra 25p for every £1 donated by a taxpayer; this could be increased to 30p or more, which would bolster charitable income significantly. There are indications that during the pandemic, the use of Gift Aid increased and so increasing the benefit from it would sustain this impact.[3] In 2021, Gift Aid income across the sector was £1.38 billion;[4] increasing the rate to 30p would raise an additional £69 million annually.

For organisations and congregations reliant on regular giving via direct debit, we recommend a concerted attempt to **link giving with the rate of inflation.** While not all givers will be able to afford to increase their giving in line with inflation, particularly in the current climate, the experience of those we heard from suggests that this is a behavioural challenge as much as an economic one. People are more likely to do so when prompted explicitly, which relatively few charities do.

There are also recommendations which relate to the current crisis more closely. For example, the idea of "warm banks" has grown in prominence in recent months, as a potential community support mechanism for those unable to afford household heating bills. This should not be seen as a long-term alternative to affordable energy costs for the majority of the population, but may be a valuable resource in what is likely to be a difficult winter. We recommend that these spaces should be viewed as the extraordinary measures that they are and operated in a targeted and strategic manner. For example, while it may be tempting for all churches and similar buildings to open as warm hubs, there may be more effective ways of ensuring all communities have access to such spaces. **Newer buildings and those with fixed-term energy deals should be prioritised** in order to minimise the cost of operating a warm hub in the community.

Those which already have high footfall from the local community should also be prioritised; the Church of England, for example, could use data already gathered on carbon emissions from previous winters as a proxy for most used church buildings and deliver support accordingly. This may mean collaboration between different denominations and groups to determine the most efficient choice of location in a particular community. Coordination should also enable communities to have a space open every day of the week through individual groups taking turns.

Collaboration with local authorities would make this even more effective by identifying geographic areas at greatest need of warm bank provision, or which do not have other public spaces like libraries to access. This is particularly critical in rural areas, where public services are spread thinly and public transport not forthcoming. In those areas, it may be strategic to operate multiple buildings as warm hubs to improve access, whereas in more densely populated urban areas these could be consolidated. For example, Cornwall is identified as one of the areas of the UK where heating bills are highest relative to average income,[5] but also fits this description of an area where community spaces may be scattered at great distances apart – what we might call "heating deserts". Recent research showed that in Shetland, 96% of the population are expected to be in fuel poverty by the new year, with a salary of £104,000 needed to avoid this.[6] This again highlights the way that areas with high energy costs due to their geography are often also those with lower wages, which compounds the problem. These areas should be prioritised for any intervention.

In order for these spaces to operate effectively, however, we acknowledge that there is a need for both **additional funding and additional volunteer support**, neither of which are easy to come by in the current climate. There is at present a piecemeal system of grant funding for charities and community groups, provided by some national institutions and local authorities. This is to be welcomed, but is unlikely to be enough without action from a structural level to address the scale of the energy bills facing these groups. By its own admission, the Church Commissioners' package is generous but not sustainable over the longer term. It would be better to mediate this through reducing bills upfront rather than finding ways to fund them once they have risen.

We recommend the **introduction of a cap on energy prices on community spaces**, similar to that applied to household rates. This would substantially mediate the effects of rising bills on community institutions and mean that more of them are able to stay open throughout the winter. This could also apply to small businesses like pubs, which face many of the same challenges as church halls but which also represent key public spaces in many communities and should be preserved. Exemption from business rates for small businesses and non-profit organisations would add to this. In addition to emergency measures introduced during this crisis, a permanent cap applied to these spaces would avoid the insecurity and anxiety that has arisen from this in future years as well. Similarly, the introduction of a social tariff for energy prices – similar to that currently operating for water bills – would regulate the costs for lower income households and community spaces alike, providing a significant level of security currently not afforded.

These recommendations offer means to ensuring security for charities and faith groups through the current crisis, as well as establishing greater stability and rootedness for communities over the longer term. They are primarily aimed at national and

> **These recommendations offer means to ensuring security for charities and faith groups through the current crisis, as well as establishing greater stability and rootedness for communities over the longer term.**

local government, with solutions at the level of third sector and faith organisations, rather than individuals and households.

For faith communities, it is important to recognise the increased precarity that will arise at an organisational level as a result of the increased insecurity of the individuals that make up the congregation. In essence, the resilience of local communities cannot rest on the church because the church itself is an insecure institution composed of individuals whose lives are also insecure. We suggest that this is not necessarily a negative reality, but rather a recognition of the changing situation of the church in society and something we might adapt to. We suggest that it would be beneficial for churches and faith communities **to think about insecurity as a longer-term reality**, while still working to reduce it, and to consider how it might impact their worship and practice, particularly those for whom it is a newer experience.

We contend that the imperative seen throughout the Old Testament to care for the widow, orphan, and foreigner, who are inherently in positions of insecurity, remains relevant today. There are still whole swathes of our society who experience the same insecurity, through both economic instability and a disconnection from community. Policy makers and faith leaders alike should take seriously the issue of insecurity, prioritising the security of communities as well as their prosperity.

Recommendations

1. Charity Commission for England and Wales, *Guidance: Sales leases transfers or mortgages: what trustees need to know about disposing of charity land* (2022). Available at: www.assets.publishing.service.gov.uk/government/uploads/system/uploads/attachment_data/file/622147/CC28.pdf

2. Community Land Trusts, *What Is A Community Land Trust?* (2022). Available at: www.communitylandtrusts.org.uk/about-clts/what-is-a-community-land-trust-clt/

3. NCVO data.

4. Hargrave, R, "Gift Aid income 'stable' at £1.38bn despite pandemic", *Civil Society*, 4 November 2021. Available at: www.civilsociety.co.uk/news/gift-aid-income-stable-at-1-38bn-despite-pandemic.html

5. Vigar, T, "Cornwall residents could be spending a fifth of their salaries on energy bills by October", *Cornwall Live*, 4 August 2022. Available at: www.cornwalllive.com/news/cornwall-news/cornwall-residents-could-spending-fifth-7420744

6. Stout, J, "Oil tankers line Shetland's horizon, but islanders face bitter fuel poverty", *Open Democracy* (2022). Available at: www.opendemocracy.net/en/shetland-energy-crisis-fuel-poverty-oil-gas/

Theos – enriching conversations

Theos exists to enrich the conversation about the role of faith in society.

Religion and faith have become key public issues in this century, nationally and globally. As our society grows more religiously diverse, we must grapple with religion as a significant force in public life. All too often, though, opinions in this area are reactionary or ill informed.

We exist to change this

We want to help people move beyond common misconceptions about faith and religion, behind the headlines and beneath the surface. Our rigorous approach gives us the ability to express informed views with confidence and clarity.

As the UK's leading religion and society think tank, we reach millions of people with our ideas. Through our reports, events and media commentary, we influence today's influencers and decision makers. According to *The Economist*, we're "an organisation that demands attention". We believe Christianity can contribute to the common good and that faith, given space in the public square, will help the UK to flourish.

Will you partner with us?

Theos receives no government, corporate or denominational funding. We rely on donations from individuals and organisations to continue our vital work. Please consider signing up as a Theos Friend or Associate or making a one off donation today.

Theos Friends and Students

- Stay up to date with our monthly newsletter
- Receive (free) printed copies of our reports
- Get free tickets to all our events

£75/ year for Friends   **£40**/ year for Students

Theos Associates

- Stay up to date with our monthly newsletter
- Receive (free) printed copies of our reports
- Get free tickets to all our events
- Get invites to private events with the Theos team and other Theos Associates

£375/ year

Sign up on our website:
www.theosthinktank.co.uk/about/support-us